Free Traffic
For Broke Marketers

Presented By Mason Ramm
(Publisher) Of

Legal Notice/Disclaimer:

There is no guarantee of success, traffic and/or that you will make money, either written or implied. The author /publisher specifically disclaims any personal liability, loss, or risk incurred, as a consequence of acting on, undertaking or relaying any advice or information presented herein.

While all attempts have been made to verify information provided in this publication, neither the author nor the publisher assumes any responsibility for errors, omissions or contradictory interpretation of the subject matter herein.

This publication is not intended to be used as a source of legal or business advice. Please remember that the information contained may be subject to varying state and/or local laws or regulations that may apply to the user's particular practice.

The purchaser or reader of this publication assumes responsibility for the use of these materials and information. Adherence to all applicable laws and regulations, both federal, state, and local, governing professional licensing, business practices, advertising and any other aspects of doing business in the US or any other jurisdiction is the sole responsibility of the purchaser or reader.

The author and publisher of this publication assumes no responsibility or liability whatsoever on behalf of any purchaser or reader of these materials. Any perceived slights of specific people or organizations is unintentional.

Information in this report is provided solely for the user's information and, while thought to be accurate, is provided strictly "as is" and without warranty of any kind, either expressed or implied. We will not be liable to you for any damages, direct or indirect, or lost profits or data arising out of your use of information provided in this report.

Every effort has been made to accurately represent our product and its potential. Please remember that each individuals success depends on his or her background, dedication, desire and motivation. As with any business or money making endeavor or venture, there is no guarantee of success.

Proceeding Beyond This Point Constitutes Your Acceptance Of This Legal Notice/Disclaimer.

Dear Reader,

Here's how it goes with most new marketers – it happened to me *exactly* like this – see if it rings a bell with you. It might even be that this is the stage you're currently at…..

I quickly realized the potential of internet marketing. Not least because I could see people around me making a lot of money, or at least making more than enough to quit work and go full-time.

The initial excitement I felt has never left me. I vividly remember working late into the night creating my first ebook, then once that was finished the REAL work began – learning how to build a simple website, use a hosting account, register for Paypal and Clickbank, ftp my files to my hosting account, put a payment button (that actually worked) in the right place on my website and struggle to write a half decent sales page.

Once it was ALL done, my website went live and I waited to get rich.

…and waited

…and waited.

I didn't make a SINGLE sale from my first attempt at product selling. I had neglected one of the most important parts of the whole process. Getting people to look at my website – TRAFFIC!

When I realized I needed traffic I got a BIG shock. The cost of paying for any sort of advertising was way out of my tiny budget's reach, and the time spent on some of the traditional methods of traffic generation would have meant I had to quit my job to have time to do it!

So I had to find my own way. I had to find what worked for me. Which methods were most effective among the masses of conflicting advice I read about on the forums?

Well what I found was **free traffic for broke marketers.**

And while not everything you're about to read is groundbreaking or new, I CAN tell you that it works for me, and best of all it's FREE.

When newcomers to Internet Marketing first get involved in the entire process of creating their own products, designing sales or landing pages and trying to stimulate enough traffic to make sales, they often get lost.

Losing your way in the Internet wasteland is not a failing on your part, but a by-product of information overload and a lack of the specific steps you need to take to accomplish your goal. We've all been there.

This eBook is designed with you in mind, the newcomer to the most critical part of Internet Marketing...driving traffic to your sites. If you do not understand the powerful options available to you for generating a traffic flow of interested visitors, you will not make many, if any, sales.

The entire focus of this guide is how to generate FREE traffic with any or all of the successful techniques presented here. You are advised to try one method at a time and not too get scattered trying to tweak and master too many things at the same time.

--- * ---

The worst kept secret – article marketing.

Writing articles and submitting them to article directories is a simple, but very powerful and effective way to create interest and generate traffic to your site. Best of all, it's free.

For years, most successful online marketers and many marketing offline too, have used article submission as a way to draw attention to their products and send interested traffic their way.

Basically how it works is that you write interesting (hopefully) articles. You submit them to article directories for other people to use freely on their sites, blogs and in their written works. The condition is that they have to use the article as it is – they're not allowed to change it – and at the bottom you have included a link back to your own website, product or blog. When people read the article, and if they like it, they'll possibly click on the link and you'll get free traffic to your website.

Here's some steps to follow if you fancy giving this a try.

- **Before you do anything else, consider your topics for your articles.**

    If you want to have your articles accepted by the directory admin and published for everyone to find, you have to have fresh, new content. It's fine to use PLR (Private Label Rights) material that you've bought or gotten hold of for free but make sure you rewrite it slightly or add to it. Don't be tempted to use it as it comes because it's highly likely that other people have bought the same PLR and have submitted it to the same directory.

    Unfortunately, there are hundreds, or even thousands, of other people using the same PLR articles you have. Your goal is to be different than the rest of the pack, not a clone of the multitudes.

If you have a specific niche you want to promote, pick a topic related to that particular niche that would interest your readers and write 300-700 words on
that particular subject.

For example: If gardening is your passion, your topics could be:

- Growing vegetables
- Raising roses
- Herb gardens
- 100 things to do with zucchini (make up your own jokes!)
- 100 Garlic secrets
- How to send your garden pests to your neighbor's yard (my favorite)

You get the idea...list everything you know about your passion and you have the topics for your articles. Don't be afraid to have a little fun with article topics. Write like you are talking to your neighbor or a friend and denying that you sent the snail army his way.

If you're into Internet Marketing, think about what you are selling online...ebooks, software, memberships...and the benefits of buying your products. Each benefit could be turned into an article to send you directed traffic, which is what you want.

Another example: If you are selling ebooks on how to solve a problem, your articles could have just enough information about that problem and its solution to make your interested readers want to know more, sp in this case the link at the bottom of your article would be to a 'full size' book on the subject.

- **Do not make your articles one long, fancy ad for your products. These *won't* get published.**

Newsletter and blog publishers are hungry for new content to present to their readers. You don't have to reinvent the wheel, but you do have to rewrite it some to make it interesting and useful to the publisher's readers.

That means:

- **Provide fresh looks at old ideas**

    Not much new exists today that cannot be restated or reordered to make it a new article with great possibilities for traffic generation.

    The browsing public is starving for information on any topic imaginable. You can find out what they are looking for in your niche by using any keyword generator. You will know how many people looked for your specific keywords last month.

    If you plan on using articles to drive traffic to your products, wouldn't that be handy information to have BEFORE you start writing articles?

- **Offer new solutions to old problems we all share**

    There's more than one way to fix a stuck drawer, make your car shine like a jewel, remove the mystery stain on your kid's new shirt or get better phone service.

    Problems are everywhere. We all have more than we need and the reading public is no different. A list that promises a new way to overcome everyday hassles is usually warmly welcomed by newsletter publishers because anyone can relate to the information.

    Be creative and your articles will be appearing all over the Internet. If you have a humorous story about how you discovered the solution or had to create it, add it to the article. Do not write in a technical, stilted manner. Just make sure your solutions work. If you have enough solutions to the same problem to make several articles, do it.

- **Create a new list of steps to get something done**

    People everywhere love hand-holding and step-by-step lists of techniques or processes to make their life easier, especially when they are dealing with some of the new, popular technical aspects of the Web 2.0 social media.

These articles are in every article directory and people flock to them. Most want to know how to master these vague processes that do so much "wizardry" on web pages.

If you know how to master one of the processes that baffle so many people, you have just struck article gold. Write a step-by-step tutorial that starts at the beginning and finishes with a completed process.

You see examples in your email box all day long with titles like *"5 Secrets To Unlock _____,"* *"Easy PHP Scripts to _____"* or *"How to _____."*

Read some articles in any directory on your niche topic and get ideas for new articles on the same subject. Ideas are **not** copyrightable and any that pop into your head while you're reading the competition are yours to use as you wish.

- **Share your grandmother's family secret biscuit recipe (ask her first though)**

    A lot of useful information and techniques are fading away as the new generations flock to the "new stuff" like hungry seagulls on a deserted beach.

    Our heritage is full of the ways our grandparents or great-grandparents used to create safe havens for their families and most of it is quietly crumbling into archival dust. Those methods can be resurrected from old bibles, handwritten cookbooks or the memories of your aging relatives and made into articles and even ebooks that would be popular today.

Public domain repositories are goldmines of the processes and traditions from your past the made today possible. The information found there can be freely used, rewritten to suit yourself, broken into short articles or several ebooks or published as is. Check the laws for your own country first.

You can find almost anything you need in the public domain, like software, pictures, movies, plays, poetry, ebooks, music, artwork or technical works to name a few. A Google search for "public Domain" will fill your folders with more resources than you will ever need.

Here's a few to get you started:

In the US:

- Project Gutenberg - http://www.promo.net/pg
- Project Bartleby - http://www.bartleby.com
- Christian Classics Ethereal Library - http://www.ccel.org

In the United Kingdom:

- Free Classic Literature Library - http://www.classic-literature.co.uk/
- British Library Collection - http://blpc.bl.uk/collections/wider/etexts.html
- The Morgue File - http://www.morguefile.com/archive
- Virtual Library - http://www.sdst.org/shs/library/cfimages.html
- Newspaper Archives - http://www.sdst.org/shs/library/catalogs.html

- **Every Article Directory has submission guidelines that have to be followed to the letter.**

    Do not assume that every article directory has the same guidelines. If you do not follow those posted guidelines, you will not get published. New article acceptance is **not** done by robots, but by human beings looking for violations of their policies.

Articles submission services will, for a fee, submit your articles to hundreds of directories, but they will not check for submission guidelines for each directory. That is your responsibility.

For example, if the guidelines state that the title of your article has to have the first letter of each word capitalized, they will not accept articles with even one word not capitalized.

Acceptable: *"The Real Secret Of Internet Marketing"*
Not Acceptable: *"The Real Secret of Internet Marketing"*

Here's a few popular article directories where you can submit your articles:

- Ezine Articles - http://www.ezinearticles.com/
- Article Dashboard - http://www.articledashboard.com/
- Article Marketer - http://www.articlemarketer.com/

Don't forget to read the Submission Guidelines and follow them to the letter.

--- * ---

Link building For Success

Every Internet Marketer is focused like a hungry shark on increasing their page rank and improving their Search Engine Optimization (SEO) and, if you are a serious marketer, you might be, too. Your attention will be sharply focused on "backlinks," their individual quality and how those backlinks appear to Google's army of robot spiders when compared in their current algorithm.

Let's start with **"backlinks."** They are links on other websites directed back to your website. Both the popularity and the importance of your website is gauged by how many other website owners consider a link to your site worthwhile. All of this is done in the name of Search Engine Optimization...or getting Google and other search engines to love your website.

But, don't run off gathering up as many links as you can from other marketers. Google is more interested in "quality" backlinks to your website than any others. Those quality backlinks would be backlinks from websites with similar content to yours. It's all a game of relevancy, from Google's point of view, and has a lot to do with the success of your website and marketing efforts.

A search engine calculates the keyword relevancy for a site and that calculation is strictly based on the percentage of related content found at either end of the link. For example, if your content is all about writing and selling ebooks, and the links from other sites have nothing to do with writing and selling ebooks, they will not be considered important to your relevancy and you will lose page rank or be totally ignored by the spiders.

There's several ways to accomplish this balancing act with the search engines and to stay out of SEO trouble while you're doing it. More than one seedy webmaster has been banished to Google Hell for trying to manipulate links to get a higher ranking, which is why Google tightened the criteria in the first place.

> **Word of caution:** **Do not get involved with "Link Farms."**
>
> Link Farms, according to Wikipedia, are *"a collection of intentionally-interlinked pages, designed to fool search engines that use Page Rank or a similar algorithm, into believing that the pages are more important than they really are. Google is known to employ a link farm detection algorithm, which penalizes those pages determined to be a link farm."*

There's lots of ways to virtually shoot yourself in the foot online without irritating Google, so why add it to the list?

Backlinks are great ways to get visitors to your website. That old chestnut, *"Build it and they will come!"* has no meaning in the virtual world of Internet Marketing. If no one knows you're there and what you're doing, they will **NEVER** find you.

One way to attract attention and the resulting free traffic, is with reciprocal link exchanges, as long as those links are "quality" links and from other sites with content or focus similar to yours. You will have to learn to check out your link partners and avoid any with pages full of unrelated links or links to what Google labels **"Bad Neighborhoods."**

If Google devalues a site because of the **"bad company"** it keeps, or the **"bad neighborhood"** in hangs out in, your site will get devalued also and dropped in Page Rank if you are linked to it, or worse, just ignored by the robots.

What makes a bad neighborhood?

- Sites that use **black-hat techniques** to drive traffic
- Sites with many, **many pages of outbound links**
- Sites with pages of **no content** usually are just storage sites for thousands of links of poor quality and will certainly have Google snorting fire.

You will have to stay constantly vigilant to make sure you are not linked to a *"bad neighborhood."* You are in control of whom you link to and that has to be your main focus. You cannot control who links to you, **but the search engines will**

punish you if you link out to a *"bad neighborhood."*

A search for the term "bad neighborhood," with quotes, will turn up several **free tools** you can access to uncover any sites that might be harmful to your own linkbuilding efforts.

There are certain industries that seem to be involved in using spam and link farming techniques that you need to be aware of before you start building your links. Two major players in this field are the pharmaceutical and adult industries. Unless your business is in some aspect of those two industries, you would be well advised to avoid them entirely.

While inbound links to your site are good to have, quality outbound links to other high-quality or authority sites definitely will help your rankings considerably. Just remember that, in order for those outbound links to matter, they have to be within the subject field of your site.

There are a couple of things you have to consider while you are trying to get traffic and a decent Page Rank for your websites. **It is important for you to check on your links and to keep track of which sites are linking back to you.** If all the links are outbound from your site and not reciprocated with a link back, the sites on the other end of your outbound links will get all the traffic and page rank. You, on the other hand, will be considered an unimportant website.

Search on *"verifying reciprocal links,"* with quotes, and you will have a list of online tools you can use to check your site and those you've linked to for backlinks.

Another major consideration for your marketing success is the content of the **anchor text of the backlink** (what the link actually says on your site) and how it is using, or not using, the keywords relevant to your site.

For example, **"Click Here"** is totally generic and does not relate in anyway to your website. But, **"For a great recipe, visit our site,"** uses your keyword, "recipe" in this example, in the hyperlinked anchor text. Search engines love this.

There's several easy ways to generate a set of quality links for your sites. Before you do anything, though, you have to make sure you know whom your audience is and who you want to attract to your site. Once you locate your target audience, focus your link building efforts on sites within that audience.

Your major task when looking for link possibilities is to slowly build your own directory of sites with themes that complement your site's focus. These sites do not have to be exactly identical to yours, but they do have to be related in focus and content. For example, if your site is all about collecting comic books, a site that provides tips on pricing and/or preserving comic books would be a valuable link for you. Your keywords would probably be somewhat the same.

One outstanding way to find possible websites for reciprocal linking is to use the search engines to find the top sites with the same keywords you use. Use several search engines...*Google is not the only search engine on the Web*...and search on your keywords. The sites that come up in the first five or six places are websites **the search engines consider important** and have ranked them accordingly. Your next move is to visit those sites and contact the webmasters and ask for a link.

Some will decline, if their site is in high competition with yours. Don't take it personally. It is just business. But some will accept, especially if you offer a link back to their site. When that happens, you just added a high quality backlink to boost your value with the search engines.

From time to time, you will get offers for a link trade with sites that say they've already placed your link on their links page. Check that out carefully. If they get a link from you and do not have one back to your site on their links page, they are only helping themselves to your traffic and not reciprocating.

Another thing to check out is whether or not they have a link on their **home page** to their link pages. If they don't, decline the invitation. Google won't spider the link page and the link would be totally worthless to you.

When you are looking at link pages on other sites, avoid linking to any that have multiple link pages crammed full of links of all types. If you remember the discussion above about Link Farms, you will recognize what you are looking at.

> **Another caution:** Do not link to pages with a zero page rank. That link will do nothing for your own page rank and you might be linking in a bad neighborhood or to a website that has been banned by Google.

As discussed earlier, a simple but powerful way to get quality backlinks is to write and submit articles on your niche to webmasters who publish newsletters focused on your niche.

Not only will they appreciate new content for their readers, but also you will provide yourself with a backlink that means something to Google. How? Your author's box will have a link back to your site, along with a sentence or two about you. Article marketing is viral and provides a necessary resource for other marketers and publishers.

Smart marketing starts when you first think about your website. The first choice you have to make is your list of keywords that govern how your site is perceived, listed and ranked. You can use several free keyword tools to see how many people are searching for information using your keywords.

A simple search for "keyword," (no quotes), or *"keyword search tool,"* will return several online keyword search tools you can use to analyze your keywords, generate new keywords and compare keyword density on your websites.

Here are three **FREE**, good ones to start with:

- Google AdWords Keywords Tool
- https://adwords.google.com/select/KeywordToolExternal
Because this is a Google tool, you will have the benefit of using the largest search user base in the universe. You can view a 12-month historical trend or simply analyze a site or page with keyword suggestions.

- Yahoo! Search Marketing - http://searchmarketing.yahoo.com/
(formerly known as **Overture)** This tool is free, quick to set up and easy to use. This service offers general or regional marketing.

- [Overture Keyword Selector Tool](http://inventory.overture.com) - http://inventory.overture.com
  With this free service, just go to the site and enter in a search term. Overture automatically returns related searches including your term and the estimated number of times that term was searched for in the previous month.

When you've got your keywords selected to provide the most benefit to your marketing plan, put them to work for you immediately:

- Use them in your website title
- Sprinkle them throughout your sales page text
- Definitely put them in the description of your page in your HTML code
- Make sure they are in the metatags of your source code

Everything about virtual marketing depends on the value of your keywords. The search engines use them to index your site and evaluate your site contents. Customers use them to find the information they need. Your competitors use them to draw more traffic than you do.

Now that you've got your keywords in your source code's where they need to be, let's move on to **building your link pages** with the intention of making the most use of its subtle power for your marketing efforts.

The question now is **"What Do You Put On Your Link Pages?"**

Build a link page on your website giving other webmasters permission to link to yours and make it super easy for them to do it. Put everything they will need right at their fingertips and make it easy to find. If you offer several choices for links, make sure there's enough separation between them so it is easy to see where one ends and another begins…don't jam things together.

- **Provide HTML code for your link so they can just copy and paste it on their link page**

  The easier it is to add your link to their pages, the more likely it will get added by webmasters. If it is a hassle, they won't bother to use your link.

  Before you post the code on your link page for the webmasters to access, make sure your URL is correct. **Check it!…Check it!…**

Check it! How stupid would you feel if you published an incorrect link for your own site? I know because I've done it.

- **Make sure your keywords are in the linking HTML code**

    This gives your link a double whammy...the keywords will be picked up by the search engines for people searching those phrases and your link will seem more important to the indexing spiders.

- **Small banners or buttons with your linked code attached are always attractive for those with a taste for graphics over text**

    On a page of text links small colorful banners or buttons, hyperlinked to your site, are attention-getters and might just make your link stand out in the crowd. Some webmasters prefer graphic links.

    One thing you absolutely need to add to a graphic link is the HTML "Alt" tag. Search engine spiders do not recognize graphics. They only read text, so the explanation located in that tag will be enough for the spider to index it.

    If you decide to follow this suggestion, do not go overboard and add animation and flashy effects to the banner...just a tasteful, colorful button or small banner is all that is needed.

- **Put a description with each link on your links page.**

    This looks professional and keeps your page from looking like a Link Farm to the search engine spiders.

    Put a link to your link pages on your home page and any other pages you have on your website so your visitors and the search engines, can find it.

Remember that those indexing spiders check your links to determine value and legitimacy. If you have links going out to link farms or bad neighborhoods, you will be punished by the search engines...sort of "birds of a feather..." mentality.

Now that you have a good-looking link page, let's take a look at how to ask for links on other webmaster's pages.

Before you make any contacts, search on your keywords to find sites with decent page rank and similar content, but not directly in competition with your page. Visit the page and take note of how a link to your page would be a welcome resource for that page's visitors.

A webmaster would be more interested in adding your link when he discovers that you have visited his page and noticed the possible benefits your link would add to his site.

When possible, use the telephone, old fashioned it may be, but a personal phone call from you to a webmaster is likely to get more consideration than a "cold call" email. Introduce yourself and mention that you had been on his site and would be interested in placing a link on his site.

If a phone call is not possible, compose a polite email, mentioning some of the parts of his site that you liked and how a link from you would benefit his site visitors. This technique is far better than an email that just asks for a link without providing any justification for it and is a dead giveaway that you've never been on the site.

If you are targeting an ezine in your niche, the best way to get links is through the author's box in articles submitted either to article directories or directly to ezine publishers. The first chapter in this ebook discusses article submission directly, but it is so virally powerful that it deserves another mention here.

By now, you should have some good techniques to spread your reputation and news of your website across the Web without spending a cent. With Internet Marketing, FREE does not mean useless or without power. Every technique mentioned so far and the hyperlinked online resources mentioned are for you to freely to use...no cost.

Let's move on to a couple of other powerful FREE options for your marketing arsenal.

--- * ---

Newsletters & Ezines

Hundreds of webmasters publish niche newsletters or ezines on a regular basis, weekly or monthly, to lists that probably range in the tens of thousands of avid readers. Their publications deliver fresh content to their subscribers and the need for that fresh content is endless. Here's where you come in.

When you can provide quality information to those publishers in the form of articles in the 300-500 word range you will broadcast your name and webpage link across the Internet almost instantly. If you keep submitting quality articles, you will quickly be considered an authority or expert on the niche subjects you write about.

This is no exaggeration and is one of the quickest and most effective ways to drive traffic for free.

To be successful at this you have to consider your audience first.

- **Who are they?**
    - Collectors?
    - Parents?
    - Senior Citizens?
    - Crafters?
    - Gardeners?
    - Internet Newbies?
- **What do they want to know?**

- How to do _____ ?
- How to fix _____ ?
- How to understand _____ ?
- How to make money online?

- **What problems do they need solutions for?**
    - Technical computer problems?
    - Fixing web page disasters?
    - Repairing marketing mistakes?
    - Removing stains from clothing?
    - How to make a better cup of coffee?

- **What are their passions, hobbies or interests?**
    - What is their niche focus?
    - What is missing from their enjoyment and use of their niche?

- **Where do they hang out?**
    - Forums?
    - Blogs?
    - Internet Cafes?
    - Chat rooms?

With that information, you can directly address the problems and passions of the newsletter's membership and increase the value of your article submissions to the webmaster. To begin with, it sounds like an impossible task, but simple research will uncover amazing details about a webmaster's community.

Pay particular attention to the comments made by the subscribers. They usually reveal a lot about themselves without even realizing it. For example, off topic comments are very revealing if you know what you are looking at:

- "I had to spend the morning getting rid of ants in the kitchen..."
- "I took my kids to the beach yesterday and when I got home..."
- "My sales page isn't working like I wanted it to work and I don't know what to do about it."

You get the idea. People who feel like they belong to a newsletter's community, virtual or not, start getting chatty and, sure, a lot of it will not have any value for your purposes. But the real value is the "accidental" listing of problems for you to solve or address with additional information. Learn to read with an eye for holes you can fill with your writing...Marketing gold and Free traffic gold rush.

Writing for the Internet is not like anything you ever learned in high school. Newsletter and ezine subscribers want to feel like they belong to a community and are not just an email address with a valid credit card to the publishers. In order to instill that sense of belonging, articles, ebooks and the actual newsletter have to be written in a friendly, conversational manner.

Write like you are talking to your friend or a neighbor. Explain your points in plain words and not in the stilted, strained manner found in some ebooks and articles. **Just talk**, but do it with your fingers and your keyboard.

Before you submit directly to any webmaster or publisher, subscribe to their publication and read it. Check out back issues in the archives. Read the comments in several that interest you.

Look for questions or problems that you can address and do so, either with a good comment or later, with a short report or article that you submit to the webmaster. Problems needing solutions are free goldmines of fresh content for you to mine.

BONUS: Get FREE Internet Marketing Products, Tools & Resources at: www.GiveAwayClub.net

==One effective way to get free newsletter publicity is to take one of those problems that needed solutions and turn it into a short report, 4-10 pages, and offer it to the webmaster as a free bonus or gift to his subscribers. Of course, the report will be branded with your details, particularly your name and your link to your site.==

Webmasters are very interested in free bonuses for their subscribers and would welcome your gift offer if it is about some aspect of their niche and of real value to their subscribers. Being able to offer free, fresh content to their subscribers raises the value of being a member of their newsletter and increases subscriber loyalty. If you can provide that content, you will benefit by having your link in front of thousands of subscribers in a few days. This is definitely a Win-Win-Win situation for you, the webmaster and the subscribers.

As your reputation grows built by your articles and free reports, webmasters will come looking for you (the smaller the niche, the quicker this will happen).

Their subscribers will follow your link to your page, looking for more information or resources. You will become an authority or expert in the newsletter's niche and your traffic will increase dramatically. You will be the darling of the search engines, where rewarding fresh content with higher page rank is their main task.

Always remember, writing articles and for ezines is not your main task – driving traffic.

--- * ---

Using Forums To Increase Traffic

You can find forums all over the Web with a focus on almost any niche subject you can think up. By far, the Internet Marketing, "Make Money At Home" subject is the most popular forum focus today and probably for more than several thousand tomorrows, too.

It is easy to find forums with targeted traffic for any niche that exists. Just use any search engine, enter your niche keywords, and stand back. Find one or two forums that interest you and join. Quite a few forums are free to join. Some of them on the highly popular Internet Marketing subjects are fee-based, but do not discount the free ones for your traffic-generating marketing.

In fact I've had better results from free forums.

Members of free forums have the same questions, problems and needs that fee-based forum members have. They also have credit cards and will buy products that seem useful to them or products that provide resources they need.

The first task you have as a brand new forum member is to introduce yourself to the other members. Most forums have a "New Member" category that is used for introductions and soft self-promotion...who you are...where you live...what you do...or what's your interest or experience with the niche you just joined.

Create a short, friendly bio covering the pertinent details and post it in the appropriate category on each forum you join.

Create a signature (Sig) that appears at the end of **every** forum post you make and on any email or private message you may send. All it needs is your screen name or real name and a statement or two, with your link, that will get clicks from any interested forum member. Here are a couple of examples:

"Tom Jones
Need a song? Contact Songwriter (http://www.songs4u.com)
for music written just for you!"

"Lady Bug
Got ants in your pants? Visit Garden Solutions
(http://www.gardensolutions.com)
for "Going Green" solutions to a nasty garden problem."

(The links in the two examples are not valid, but used to illustrate the point being made)

Whatever you decide your niche is, add your linked signature to every single posting or email you send, even emails to your mother. A carefully constructed signature is totally viral and will zip around the Web without you having to think about it again.

For example, let's say you send your mother a good joke or recipe and she sends it along to friends and relatives, who do the same thing. Most will just click forward and your signature file is going along with it. There is no way to tell who will see your sig and need the information or support promised there. This is a very effective and free marketing soft sell that keeps on working. Do not discount it.

Now that you have created your online personality, let's take care of the rest of your forum marketing techniques.

Read every category in your new forum. Get to know the moderators and their style of commenting. Learn who the strongest members are and what they post for questions or answers. When you have a good feel for the focus and tone of the community you just joined, start asking questions of your own or posting solutions. Offer links to free resources others need and links to free online processes some need, like keyword verifiers, etc.

Be supportive and gradually become a reliable source of good, clean information ...a valued community member. What you are doing here is building your reputation and creating a credibility that will carry your where you want to go with your online marketing projects.

Most marketing forums have an Announcement category where you can drop the mannerly approach and deliberately market your products. Before doing it, though, read the postings carefully to see how it is done on that specific forum and copy the methods with your own promotional method.

Another very powerful way to get attention for your products is to offer the forum members something free...a short report, ebook, piece of free software, a set of articles you've written (with your sig imbedded) that they can use for their own purposes. Make sure your free gift is worthwhile and useful. Be ready to answer questions about your gift, so make sure you use it before giving it away.

Don't forget when you have a product launch, a couple of hours posting on the forums can greatly add to your sales by just including your sig link in each post.

Try it...you'll like the response you get and the increase in traffic. It's all free!

--- * ---

Using Search Engine Optimization (SEO)

Making sure your website is popular with BOTH search engines AND customers can take some doing..

Submitting your site to the search engines and waiting for business is not very effective with Internet Marketing. You have to learn new techniques and put them to good use in order to build your online presence and climb the slippery steps of page rank.

Search engine optimization, or SEO, is the term used for getting top rankings in the major search engines. On the surface it sounds simple enough, but, in reality, it is hard work that will achieve real benefits for your business if done correctly. Let's face it; nothing of any value just magically falls in your lap.

SEO is an ongoing process with several distinct steps that, if followed and completed in a timely manner, will lead you to success. A good SEO plan will bring you a better return on your investment (ROI) than most other plans, especially online. In fact, SEO has been called "the most effective form of online marketing."

Let's get down to it.

Your goal here is to generate free traffic and build your list of customers to market to. There's several ways to do this and they all come down, once again to keyword selection, manipulation and research.

Shortcut – You can play with and tweak SEO until you drop dead of old age. It's the same old thing though – the first 20% of your SEO will bring in 80% of the profits. I personally don't mess with it too much.

Here are the basic steps that work for me.

Selecting Your Keywords

Choosing the right keywords is the first and most crucial task to be completed for your website. You have to hit a balance between really competitive keywords and those that are not so popular or competitive.

If no one is searching for information using your keywords, you will not have any customers show up at your site. If your keywords are wildly popular as search terms, the competition will prevent your rise to the top.

And just to make it *more* complicated, you must choose keywords that relate to the buyers you are trying to attract to your site. It isn't hard to attract curious browsers with cryptic headlines or questions that stir curiosity, but you want to attract visitors interested in buying what you are offering.

Sound impossible? Think you need to become a mind reader?

Not quite.

There is a simple solution to guide you through your first SEO minefield. Make a keyword list of relevant words that strike a balance between those that are highly competitive and those that are popular.

The best-known online service for you to select the keywords that would be best for your project is WordTracker (http://www.wordtracker.com). It will suggest keywords and order them based on popularity. Using a tool like WordTracker can save you a lot of time.

How Do You Measure Up With Your Rankings?

Nothing will happen to help you move up in the page rank quest until you know where you rank right now for the keywords you have chosen for your website and products.

Ideally you should now have a list of relevant keywords that are being searched by your future customers. Put those keywords in your webpage title, description and metatags and in several places in your sales copy, particularly in the first sentence or two, somewhere in the middle and at the end of your copy.

When you are ready to check your page rank, you can do it for FREE with the **Google PageRank Report.** This online tool will check the Google PageRank values for the list of URLs you enter into the form on the page. Once you know where you stand and why, you can put your efforts into improving your standing in the search engines.

Creating and Optimizing Your Webpage

Now we're down to the most critical part of search engine marketing. Your goal is to give the search engines what they want to find on your web pages and to be able to compete effectively in a shifting reality. How do you find out what they want to know? Read on.

Search your keywords in Google and go to the top 10 sites to see what makes them rank so high.

Study them, looking for:

- Content
- Keyword placement
- Keyword density
- Keyword counts
- Link popularity
- Word counts

While you're at it, it wouldn't hurt to make note of the use of colour, white space, graphics and testimonials on these top ten websites. You might pick up some good ideas to improve the look and feel of your own website. Copying success is a technique that's older than dirt. Do Not Plagiarize The Site's Content Though!

This task can be impossible if done manually. A Google search for "analyzing Keyword density" turned up more than a few FREE tools to do the job for me.

Uploading Your Website Pages

It is important that you upload your new page **every time** you make even the smallest change. Do not put it off until you make some more changes or until the weekend, etc. Not only will it keep your page current, but it will attract the robot spiders the search engines have scouring the Web. Change is new content to a search engine spider.

Submitting Your Website To The Search Engines

Submitting to search engines manually can be a boring, tedious process. The Web is teeming with submission services that advertise bulk submissions with one-click. Be very wary of jumping on these services. Some of these just gather email addresses and names for purposes other than legitimate Internet Marketing. Don't you get enough spam already?

To find submission services, search on "search engine submission services" and pick and chose the one you want to use. One thing to keep in mind is that there's only a few search engines that have enough traffic to spend time submitting your website to them. A Google search will come back with the Top 10 and Top 100 lists for search engines. The Top 10 would be a good target for your manual submissions.

Once you get some backlinks to your site, the robot spiders will visit your pages often and will not usually require a resubmit from you. Even so, it is a good practice to check your ranking monthly for each website you own. Search engines change their algorithms often, which might require some changes and fine-tuning for your web pages. Search engine optimization is not a technique you can do once and forget about.

The Web and the Internet Marketing scene can change in a heartbeat and, when it does, you have to be on top of it in order to stay current.

Long Tail Keywords

One of the newest concepts being used by smart marketers is called *"long tail keywords"* and they have a very specific purpose in marketing plans. Long Tail Keywords are search phrases composed of three or more words that become a very specific search phrase used by consumers just before they actually buy your product.

Most searches done by consumers are more generic and limited to one or two words, like "fishing" or "cookie recipes." They are mostly just testing the waters or looking for some information to think about. But when they are ready to buy, they will search with a shark-like focus to find exactly what they want. Those simple search terms mentioned above will become long tail keywords, like "fly fishing tackle" or "salt water rods and reels" or "chocolate chip cookie recipe books."

There's thought to be a well-defined buying process that consumers follow, whether online or offline. The first few steps in this buying process involve the customer thinking about wanting something, looking for information online with search engines, finding it and comparing features and prices just to see if they can afford it or really want it. At this point, your customers are using one or two word keywords as search terms.

When they have decided to buy something, they search once again with long tail keywords to specifically define what they want to buy. This is where you want to attract your customers to your site. You can do that by using the same methods your customers are using to find what they want to buy...long tail keywords specifically selected to draw them to your products.

There are two good benefits for you as a marketer:

- Long tail keywords or multi-word specific phrases rank better with the search engines than one or two-word generic phrases do
- People searching with long tail keywords are serious about finding the exact product they want and are more likely to become buyers

Using these new keyword phrases will require more pages on your website due to the large number of possible combinations that might pertain to your products or services. By the way, Google loves more pages on a website. It makes you look more substantial and important to the indexing spiders.

Your new pages do not have to be completely different than your other pages, but different versions of the ones you already have with a focus on a specific long tail topic.

A few changes will make all the difference in your site traffic. Make a unique title, using a different long tail keyword, for each new page. Use the same long tail keyword in the description, metatags, main headline and body content. Just don't get so specific that you do not attract the traffic you want.

Change up your focus to keep an assortment of different customers visiting your site. Create a few pages sending you traffic from more generic keywords and more pages sending you highly targeted traffic, but in smaller amounts.

This entire search engine optimization process is a delicate balancing act that can either make or break your business. It is a learning process that you can master with good research and a dash common sense.

But don't let it become an end in itself – too many marketers become obsessed with SEO and never actually do any marketing!

--- * ---

RSS – Syndicate Your Business

Another free marketing tool that is making the rounds of Internet Marketing is RSS, or "Really Simple Syndication," and, if used right, can send your sales over the moon.

This process begins when a webmaster wants to share his site's content with other web sites. The selected content is added to an RSS document and then registered with an RSS publisher. The content can be anything the webmaster wants it to be...articles, headlines, press releases or jokes and recipes, for that matter.

The ease of distribution gives this technique a very high potential to explode your site traffic and greatly improve the results of your marketing efforts. The key to success with RSS is to have useful content that informs and interests your audience. The same principles that apply to article writing apply here:

- Consider your target audience and write to them
- Keep your article short and to the point...200-300 words
- Write in a friendly, conversational manner
- Use "How to" tips and short step-by-step solutions to keep your readers interested
- Consider submitting your articles to newsletters and ezines as another source for traffic

Send press releases whenever there's a special event on your website or blog, or when you add new products or services.

A little time will be required to set up your RSS feed. You'll need a server, a database with descriptions of your content and the ability to use scripts. If you are unable to do these necessary tasks yourself, you can hire a freelancer to do the technical work.

When you have the details worked out, you submit your content for syndication to an RSS publisher, or aggregate. Most have specific categories for popular topics. You will have to make sure you submit your content to the correct category so your intended audience gets your feed.

Do not categorize yourself into a hole. If your content can be useful or interesting to different audiences, submit it to different aggregates under different categories.

--- * ---

Are Press Releases Still Good Marketing Tools?

Press releases have a definite place in offline marketing plans and some of the techniques easily overlap into online marketing efforts, with a few pros and cons that have to be addressed before you spend a lot of time on an activity that might be a bad fit for your business.

Until recently, press releases were thought of as being restricted to newspapers, radio and TV news slots. Now there are several online news sites with a lot of clout when it comes to audience numbers, like *Yahoo News* and *Google News*. RSS feeds make it so easy to syndicate news and press releases that the lowly press release has been given a new birth.

Wire services like *Business Wire*, *PR Newswire*, *PRWeb* and *Market Wire* simplify the process of populating current news content into the most popular search engines. To get an idea of the popularity of online news services are, there are reports that half of all Internet users visit an online news site every month.

For webmasters, the best thing about press releases are the incoming links that are attracted by the ease of distributing fresh content to both the media and consumers the easy syndication process for RSS feeds.

One interesting and surprising fact about online news services is that, of the top news services...*MSNBC*, *The New York Times*, *CNN*, etc., the number one online news destination for Internet users is *Yahoo! News*.

There are very specific formats for writing press releases – read the terms and conditions of each press release website you intend to use.

The best advice I can give you here is that most people think a press release says something like 'Today, internet marketer Josephine Doe released her new ebook 'how to make money polishing mushrooms'

It's not. You need to put an angle on it.

For example 'Poisonous mushrooms result in the deaths of 0.2% of all internet marketers' could be your headline followed by ….but it's a lucrative hobby if you take the risk'

Then you could get round to mentioning the book.

You see what I mean? Don't go immediately for the sale – do it subtly.

A search for "how to write a press release" will provide lessons and tips galore that you can use to prepare your press own releases. You might even find a template to use to speed up your learning curve. You can also find a good example of a press release and copy the format, making your own template to follow.

To answer the question in the headline, "Yes, press releases are an effective way to get the news out about your new product launch or change of business ownership." The scope of readership with online news services and RSS feeds is so large that to skip this marketing tool would be foolish. One well-written press release could be read by thousands of future customers.

Submitting press releases to newspapers might not be as effective a method as submitting to online syndications and news services. Just the sheer numbers using the Internet for news, shopping and information of all sorts, overshadows the effectiveness of newspaper marketing. If you submit to newspapers, your target market might not even see the press release.

--- * ---

Social Bookmarking Sites

When My Space burst on the Internet scene like a holiday fireworks spectacular, the entire Internet changed to accommodate this flashy, newcomer to the Web. Soon after, social bookmarking sites started springing up everywhere, some were just online communities with no specific focus and others had a definite niche focus.

Searching Google for a list of social bookmarking sites returned over 500 sites to visit and join. There's a social bookmarking site to attract almost every interest anyone ever had. As a marketing tool this online phenomenon has no competition because of the sheer numbers of monthly visitors to almost any of them.

Social bookmarking marketing is a method of promoting your product, brand or even yourself by making yourself and your business known across several social bookmarking sites. While this technique is not lightening fast, it is very effective and will produce traffic to your site. The key concept here is that social marketing is not designed to immediately boost your business income, but provide the visibility you need for conversions from visitor to buyer.

Digg.com is the most popular of the social bookmarking sites and the definite leader in the number of monthly visits, which is estimated by Quantcast to be 25 million unique visitors on any given month. Take a deep breath and read that again...**25 million unique visitors a month**. Tap that fountain of traffic and you would have something going on your site that would keep you awake for weeks.

One of the major benefits of marketing through social bookmarking sites and using their tags to promote your website, blog or Squidoo lenses is the backlinks you will receive when some of those 25 million visitors tag your site. Search engines love one-way inbound links and consider them an indication of the popularity of your site.

Each site has different requirements for creating your profile and for marketing your products with blogs, articles, etc. Join some that look interesting to you because of the content or amount of activity or focus. Take your time and get involved in some of the activities that make each social bookmarking site unique. When you are comfortable start submitting articles or your blog posts to the site and make it easy to make comments.

Invite your friends to join and send "shouts" to them whenever you post something new to any of the ones you joined. If you have a good giveaway, check the rules for each site and offer it as a free download to the members wherever you can.

Remember viral marketing? Think about your ebook or short report getting downloaded with your imbedded links to a few million members of Digg.com or My Space or any of the other 500 sites. Be sure to check with each social bookmarking site for the rules concerning giveaways and then take action!

Build A Blog

If you haven't build one yet it's probably because you're scared of them.

Don't be – they're one of the greatest free traffic driving tools ever. You can get a free one from Wordpress or Blogger. If you're very techy you can host it yourself.

Go look up how to do that part – the part I'm interested in, in how they work in terms of free traffic.

Blogs are like any website except they're dynamic – they're designed to be updates whereas updating a website is a pain in the backside. But that's not their best feature – their best feature is that *people who read your blog and like it can't WAIT to tell others about it.*

Seriously – I get SO much traffic to my blog because people have read it, liked it, and because it's human nature to enjoying discovering things before other people, they rush to tell them about it.

Your content will have to be good to get free traffic in this way, which is why I've not included it in the summary below – but if you enjoy writing and can put your personality across then a blog could be the best free traffic generator you ever have.

(Put links to your products on it obviously, and in the posts too)

I now target most of my traffic at my blog – it acts like a 'command centre' for all my sites and products, and has links to all of them.

Try it.

Thoughts on Free Traffic For Broke Marketers – a recap

I had to get creative when I realized I didn't have a budget of ANY kind to market my products when I first started out.

I'm glad I did because the techniques in this book are the best in terms of getting traffic to my sites and I use them FAR more than any sort of paid advertising.

The main ways I get traffic to my sites are:

1. Viral marketing – writing and distributing FREE reports and ebooks that also come with resell rights (so people can pass them on and so and and so on). I put links back to my sites in the ebooks. I've not gone into great detail about how to do this in this book purely there's not much to tell – write a report, put links in it back to your products – give it away.

2. Article marketing – the most effective way to make sure your articles get used by as many people as possible (therefore generating the most traffic) is to make them interesting. The best way to do **that** is to visit similar sites and see which articles turn YOU on. If they interest you, they'll interest others so write a similar article. If they bore you, they'll bore others so stay away.

3. Forum Posting. Don't underestimate this method. If I have a launch on my blog (or a viral report I want to give away) then I'll get stuck into the forums for a few hours. I change my sig as much as I change my underwear (uuuuuurgh) and every time I have a new launch I post on the forums. Don't forget when you change your sig, on most forums it automatically changes on every post you've ever written too (posts are GREAT for getting picked up by search engines so make sure you use long

term keywords in your posts), so all your past posts' sigs will also point to your latest post.

4. Blog posting – post on other people's blogs – especially HUGE guru's blogs (they don't get as many comments as you might think) and make sure you leave a link back to your products. Don't do this in the body of the post – just make sure you include your website when you sign up to leave a comment and it should be automatically included at the bottom of your post.

5. Write a newsletter or Ezine and get opt-ins in exchange for it. Include links in each ezine you send out. The easiest way is to send out a simple email newsletter. Make sure you write quality content – people aren't stupid, so don't treat them as though they are – would you want an inbox full of useless ezines? (I know you already have! – so if you write a GOOD ezine you'll stand out from the crowd and get more traffic)

6. Swapping links with other site owners. Most site owners will be fine with this. But choose people on your own level. If you approach a guru he usually won't even reply to you because there's not much in it for him, and he's not your mum. If you go for someone at the same level you're at – newbie – intermediate – whatever, you've far more chance of him being more than happy to help. AND there's a strong possibility you'll make a friend AND A JV partner. I still JV with some big marketers who I've known since we both first started out.

The main thing is to just pick a couple of the above – the ones that appeal to you are the best ones to start with – and get stuck in. You'll quickly find out which ones you like and which ones you don't.

The good news is that they all work extremely well, so as your business grows you can pay outsource workers to do the ones you don't like. As you build more sites (and if you get into Internet Marketing you can be sure you will), one of the best ways of driving traffic is the simplest of all.

Put a link on your sites, that tells your readers about your OTHER sites. Sounds obvious?

You'd be surprised how many marketers forget to do this. Bye.

Hope you enjoyed reading this,

Best regards,

Mason Ramm (Publisher)

www.LittleKnownMoneyMakers.com

www.ingramcontent.com/pod-product-compliance
Lightning Source LLC
Chambersburg PA
CBHW040931180526
45159CB00002BA/696